AN INTRODUCTION TO
ROCKS AND MINERALS

DOUGAL DIXON

CHARTWELL
BOOKS, INC.

A QUARTO BOOK

This edition published by Booksales Ltd 1995
Copyright © 1992 Quarto Publishing plc

ISBN 0-7858-0547-8

Designed and produced by Quarto Inc.
The Old Brewery,
6 Blundell Street, London N7 9BH

Senior Editor Caroline Beattie
Editor Richard Jones
Designer Nick Clark
Illustrators Dave Kemp, Janos Marffy,
Rob Shone
Picture Manager Sarah Risley

Art Director Moira Clinch
Publishing Director Janet Slingsby

Produced in Australia by Griffin Colour

CONTENTS

THE SUBSTANCE OF THE EARTH

Pick up a stone. In your hand you have a piece of the Earth's crust, made up of minerals produced by the chemical reactions that formed the planet.

MINERALS – ROCK COMPONENTS

If you take a rock, any rock, and look at it through a hand lens or a microscope you will see that it is made up of a mosaic of interlocking particles. Sometimes, in rocks such as granite, these are so big that you can see them with the naked eye. These particles are the minerals, naturally occurring homogeneous solids which have been inorganically formed. They have definite chemical compositions and definite atomic structures.

When a rock forms, the chemicals organize themselves into a number of different minerals. There are hundreds of different types, each with its own particular chemical composition, but some are more common than others. Every rock is made up of a mixture of different minerals – but usually no more than half a dozen or so.

For convenience we can divide the minerals into two broad classifications – the rock-forming minerals and the ore minerals. The latter are those that usually come to mind when the word mineral is mentioned, those that can be mined and processed for a product, but they are a very minor constituent of the Earth's crust.

As we have seen, silica (SiO_2) is the most common chemical component of the Earth, so the most common rock-forming minerals are silicates – minerals containing silica. Silica can take part in complex chemical reactions and so there are many different types of silicate mineral.

The simplest silicate mineral is quartz, which is pure silica. More commonly there are metallic elements combined with the silica. Magnesium forms a high proportion of the oceanic crust, and so the magnesium-iron silicate mineral called olivine (($Mg,Fe)_2SiO_4$) is common here. Continental crust is rich in aluminum, and so continental rocks tend to be rich in the aluminum silicate minerals called the feldspars, such as orthoclase ($KAlSi_3O_8$) and albite ($NaAlSi_3O_8$).

Carbonates – compounds containing carbon – are also important rock-forming minerals. Perhaps the most important is calcite ($CaCO_3$). This tends to be unstable when exposed to the weather and so rocks containing large proportions of carbonate tend to be eroded more quickly than those containing the more robust silicate minerals.

The silicates contain metals. However, their chemical nature is such that the metals are almost impossible to remove. Olivine therefore cannot be regarded as a source of magnesium, any more than feldspar would be a useful storehouse of aluminum. Ore minerals must contain a metal that is easily extracted. Sometimes a mineral contains the metal and nothing else. Such "native ores" include gold nuggets.

Oxides – the metal combined with oxygen – are important ore minerals. Most of the iron ores are oxides, such as magnetite (Fe_3O_4) and hematite (Fe_2O_3).

A metal combined with sulfur forms a sulfide mineral, many of which are ore minerals. These include iron pyrites (FeS_2) and the lead mineral galena (PbS).

Left When we look closely at a rock we can see that it is made up of much smaller components. Sometimes they form good crystal shapes, and sometimes irregular chunks. These components are called the minerals.

Atoms and molecules

The figures in parentheses are the chemical formulas of the minerals. The smallest indivisible part of any chemical substance is the molecule, and a molecule is made up of atoms of various elements. In chemistry an element can be referred to by a symbol, usually the initial of its common name, such as S for sulfur, or, if there are more than one with the same initial, an abbreviation of its Latin name, such as Pb standing for *plumbum* – Latin for lead.

The chemical formula reflects the number of different atoms making up the molecule. Hence the chemical formula for quartz is SiO_2, which shows that each molecule consists of an atom of silica (Si) bonded to two atoms of oxygen (O). Other elements which are referred to in this book are iron (Fe), aluminum (Al), sodium (Na), potassium (K), calcium (Ca), copper (Cu), hydrogen (H), fluorine (F), berylium (Be), zircon (Z), magnesium (Mg), manganese (Mn), chromium (Cr), titanium (Ti).

Above Some minerals are economically important. These are called the ore minerals. Iron ore, for example, comes in several mineral forms, including the yellowish powdery limonite **top** and the unevenly shaped kidney ore **above**.

Left Most minerals, however, are referred to as the rock-forming minerals, since they make up the bulk of the rocks. Calcite is a common rock-forming mineral, but only rarely does it produce the well-shaped crystals seen here.

THE ROCK CYCLE AND IGNEOUS ROCKS

The surface of the Earth is continually being created and destroyed – not usually in any way that can be perceived by human observation, but over millions, tens of millions, and hundreds of millions of years. The surface is constantly being built up of masses of mineral material, and these mineral masses are just as constantly crumbling away. The masses of mineral material are called the rocks.

We recognize three different types of rocks, depending on how they are formed.

Igneous rocks
Molten material welling up from within the Earth may eventually cool and solidify. The solid mass that results is called an igneous rock.

There are two main types of igneous rock – intrusive and extrusive.

Intrusive igneous rocks form as the molten material pushes its way upward through the rocks, cutting across or squeezing between them, and solidifying before reaching the surface. If such rocks cool slowly, they will be coarse and have mineral crystals big enough to be seen with the naked eye. If they cool quickly, they will be fine-grained. Sometimes the molten mass begins to cool slowly, crystals of one mineral begin to form, and then the whole lot is thrust into another area where it cools quickly. This gives a porphyritic texture, with big crystals in a fine groundmass.

Acidic	A rock that contains more than 66 per cent silica.
Intermediate	One that contains 66 to 52 per cent silica.
Basic	One containing 52 to 45 per cent silica.
Ultrabasic	A rock that contains less than 45 per cent silica.

Extrusive rocks, on the other hand, are those that form when the liquid erupts at the surface, as from a volcano. These are always much finer than the intrusive forms. All lavas are extrusive igneous rocks.

Another way of classifying igneous rocks is by their chemical composition. They can be rich in

Right An extrusive igneous rock forms as molten material erupts from beneath the Earth's surface and solidifies, as here in the volcano Stromboli in the Mediterranean. **Left** An intrusive igneous rock solidifies underground, and we do not see it at the surface until the overlying rocks have been worn away. Here a mass of andesite protrudes from the surrounding softer rocks in Wyoming.

silica, or poor in silica. (Those that are poor in silica still have a very high proportion of silica in them, but not as high as the others.) Such a classification involves a somewhat misleading nomenclature which convention dictates that we must use.

The terms derive from an old chemical idea that rocks are the salts of some kind of "silicious acid" – total nonsense by modern understanding, but it does leave us with a useful and workable classification.

By applying both of the above classifications, and combining the grain of the rock with its chemical composition, we can start to define the most common types of igneous rock.

Intrusive acidic rock shows large crystals, many of which are quartz. Acidic rocks tend to be lightly colored, because of the presence of quartz. Basic and ultrabasic rocks are dark. There are no

ultrabasic extrusive rocks – ultrabasic rocks are rare at the Earth's surface but are thought to be the main constituent of the mantle.

	Extrusive	Intrusive
Acidic	Rhyolite	Granite
Intermediate	Andesite	Diorite
Basic	Basalt	Gabbro
Ultrabasic		Peridotite

As a rule acidic and intermediate rocks form by the solidification of molten crustal material. Basic rocks are more likely to form from molten material brought up from the mantle.

This is a simplification. The true situation is much more complex. A solidifying melt goes through many stages of a process called fractionation before it becomes an igneous rock. As the mass cools the first minerals to crystallize out are usually those relatively low in silica, such as olivine, pyroxene, and amphibole. These can then sink to the bottom of the mass leaving a liquid that has become relatively rich in silica, and this may erupt toward the surface and form acidic rocks. A liquid rising through the tubes of a volcano will find the surrounding pressure decreasing. The gassy components will fizz off, like the bubbles in champagne when the cork is popped. A volcanic eruption will be accompanied by great blasts of gas and steam, and will produce an extrusive igneous rock that has little chemical similarity to the melt that spawned it.

Something to do

Dissolve some alum, or copper sulfate in warm water to produce a concentrated solution, as you did in the crystallization experiment on pp. 22–23. Now let it cool as slowly as possible. You should see large crystals forming. Now do the same and let the solution cool quickly. The crystals should now be so small as to be indistinguishable to the naked eye. This demonstrates the difference between the grain of an intrusive and an extrusive igneous rock.

FIELD EQUIPMENT

The field geologist should be physically fit, and be able to cope with outdoor conditions. Camping should be second nature. It would be useful to have several of the outdoor skills, such as rock-climbing and mountaineering, and to be able to handle a four-wheel-drive vehicle. It is also useful to know how to ride a horse.

This all sounds as if the practical geologist should be a marine commando, or at the very least a boy scout. These backgrounds would as a matter of fact be useful for field work in the Askja Caldera in central Iceland, or on the face of the Great Rift Valley in Tanzania. However, much valuable field work can be done in accessible localities, for which you will need a minimum of preparation.

Food and clothes

Such preparation includes suitable clothes. Dress must suit locale – waterproof parkas and pants and warm underwear for cold wet regions, and light reflective clothes and sun hats for hot sunny areas. Make them old clothes – it is a dirty business. Good strong hiking boots are a must, because you will inevitably be walking over rough, rocky terrain. Much of this is common sense, applicable to any outdoor work or activity. An addition to any wardrobe would be a pair of tough gloves. Your bare hands will suffer after handling rocks all day.

Food must also be considered. It may be that your work will be done not far from some eating place, in which case there is no problem. Otherwise plan sufficient amounts of food and drink, and allow for these when packing your equipment.

Basic equipment

The equipment should be kept to a minimum, especially if you are considering bringing back specimens. A backpack full of rocks will be heavy.

Geological hammers are essential. Indiscriminate bashing at a rock-face is the sign of the amateur. Equally, you should not destroy natural habitats without good reason; do not unnecessarily destroy plants (even lichens are of scientific importance). However, you must break open a rock in order to see its true nature: any rock that has been left will be weathered on the surface and probably covered in moss or lichen. Only a fresh face will show what the rock is really like. Take a penknife as well, for separating laminae of shale or crystals of mica.

The practical geologist should wear outdoor clothes suitable for the locale and conditions. Wet and cold weather calls for waterproof garments, as on Mount Saint Helens **right**. Hot conditions, such as those in the Philippines **far right**, demand lighter clothes. In all cases good heavy boots are essential.

1 The square end of a geological hammer is for smashing open massive rocks and for tapping chisels, and the other is for splitting sedimentary beds. Perhaps the most versatile size is 2.2 lb (1 kg). **2** A sheath is handy for carrying the hammer. **3** Cold chisels, useful for more delicate splitting work. **4** Geological pins are useful for removing individual crystals or tiny fossils.

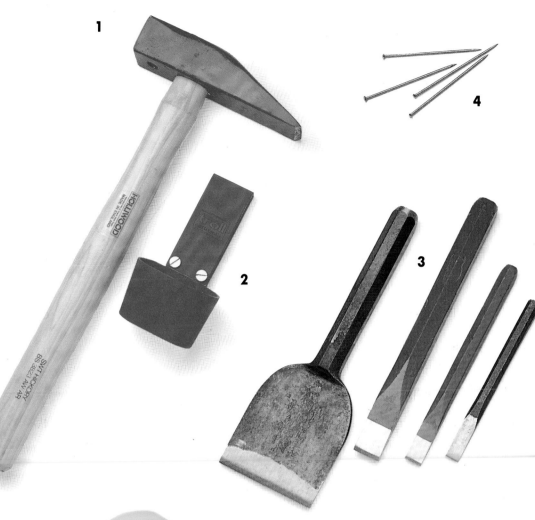

Safety tips

Safety tips

Do not try to cut corners by using a carpenter's hammer. The steel is too soft and will distort and split in no time at all. Never use the head of one geological hammer as a chisel, while hitting it with another. The hammers are not tempered during manufacture to take that sort of treatment. Accidents have been caused by flying steel shards from hammer heads splitting under such misuse.

When smashing up rocks it is important to wear a pair of goggles, to keep splinters out of your eyes. Wear a safety helmet when you are working at the bottom of a cliff face.

Although it is best to travel in groups, take a whistle, the sound of which will carry farther than your voice. Take first-aid supplies also.

USING FIELD EQUIPMENT

Smaller pieces of equipment have specialized uses.

Measuring dip

An important concept in the study of geology is that of dip. Dip is defined as the angle at which a stratum is inclined from the horizontal. The direction of dip on an exposed surface can be found by watching which way water runs down it. The angle of dip is measured by a clinometer. Such an instrument usually comprises a straight edge that is lined up against the dip of the rock, and a weight that shows the vertical. The angle of dip can be read off. Commercially produced clinometers are often combined with compasses.

Measuring strike

A compass is a valuable aid in field geology. It is, of course, used to orientate your maps. It is also used to note the strike of the outcrops. The strike can be thought of as the reciprocal of the dip. It is the line that a dipping bed makes with the horizontal – the waterline that would be formed if the bed dipped into a lake. The strike is very useful in geological mapping.

Observing and measuring

No field kit would be complete without a hand lens. The most useful magnifications are 8× or 10×, and the most convenient type is the one that folds away into a protective slot on the handle. When you find a mineral crystal or a tiny fossil worth looking at, you can whip out the lens very easily. Hold the lens close to your eye and focus it by moving the specimen toward and away from it.

Tape measures of one sort or another are essential. A very long surveyor's tape is only useful if you are doing detailed mapping and surveying. An engineer's steel tape is probably the most versatile, but a smaller angler's tape may be all you need and would be much lighter to carry.

Recording

You must record your finds. A hardcover notebook is essential. This should not be too big or it will become unwieldy – something about 4 in × 8 in (10 cm × 20 cm) is ideal. In this you can write your observations and make your sketches. Sketches may be made more conveniently on separate paper

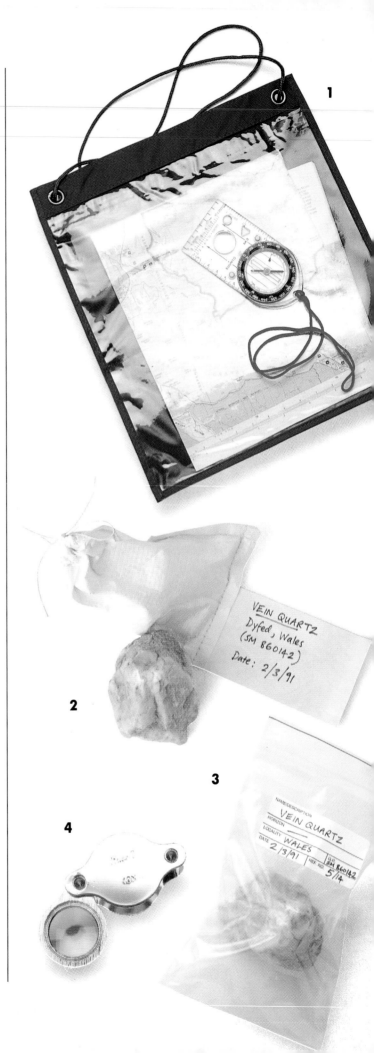

6

5

clipped to a clipboard. This can double as a map case for the maps that you will be using. Needless to say, you will need a plentiful supply of pens and pencils. Another piece of recording equipment is the camera, complete with suitable lenses and film for the type of work you are anticipating. So-called "point-and-shoot" cameras are increasingly used by professional geologists because of their simplicity and dust-protective design.

Finally, you must take wrapping materials for your specimens. Loose rocks in a bag will rattle about and become chipped and worn, ending up covered in white streaks of ground powder. Separate little linen bags are used by professional geologists, but newspaper does just as well.

The bag that carries all this must be big enough and sturdy enough to carry your equipment and your specimens as well. A canvas haversack is best. A nylon one will do, but it will wear out more quickly as the heavy items pull it into holes.

Make your own clinometer

A simple clinometer can be made by gluing a protractor to a piece of cardboard as shown. You must ensure that the horizontal of the protractor is at exactly right angles to a marked straight edge of the cardboard. Drill a hole at the protractor's center and thread a weighted line through it.

To use the clinometer, simply place the straight edge on the rock surface, ensuring that it is parallel to the dip, and read off the angle of dip on the protractor scale.

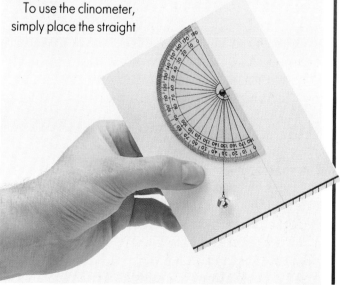

Field equipment should be kept to a minimum, but here are a few essentials. **1**. The map case should be waterproof and a handy size. The most useful compass is the kind used in orienteering. **2** and **3**. Individual labeled bags, or sheets of newspaper should be used for carrying specimens. **4**. A small hand lens is useful for on-the-spot identifications. **5**. Measuring and recording equipment should be easily portable. **6**. The bag for all this must be robust and easy to carry.

ROCK DEFORMATIONS

The movement of the continents has left its mark on their constituent rocks. Continents that have crumpled up at the edge of a subduction zone, or have ground past one another, or have crushed up against one another to form a single landmass, contain rocks that have been affected in various ways. In the extreme form, such deformation causes metamorphism , but most often rock units are folded or simply inclined.

Folded rocks

When a layered sequence of rocks is compressed, it fractures or folds. Something as apparently solid and brittle as a bed of rock can actually fold. Push a tablecloth across the table and it will develop parallel wrinkles, at right angles to the direction of push. This is similar to what happens to the rocks of the continents. In fact, extreme forms of folds, where the different waves of rock collapse over one another as deep within the Alps' center core, are called nappes (from the French for tablecloth). A few general terms are essential here. When a fold sags downward it is called a syncline. When it arches upward it is called an anticline. See the box below for further technical explanation.

We do not usually find an isolated syncline or anticline. More often they are found in a series, one following the other. The fold can be symmetrical if each flank dips at the same angle, asymmetrical if one flank is steeper than the other, or recumbent if it has turned over upon itself. Isoclinal folds are those that are so compressed that the limbs are parallel to one another.

Often the fold occurs in three dimensions, forming either a basin or a dome.

Usually we do not see a fold in its entirety in the field. We can deduce its presence by recognizing the same beds dipping in different directions not far from one another.

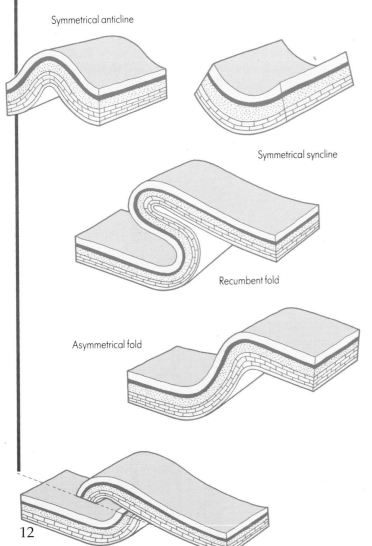

Symmetrical anticline

Symmetrical syncline

Recumbent fold

Asymmetrical fold

Left The simplest folds are symmetrical, each side being a mirror image of the other, as the anticline **top left** and syncline **top right** Intense sideways pressure forms, in turn, asymmetric and recumbent folds, finally shearing off the limb of the fold as a thrust.

Above In nature, folds are rarely simple. It is unusual to find the textbook syncline and anticline in isolation. In this example, pressure from left to right has twisted the strata into a recumbent fold at this locality in the Cape Fold Belt in South Africa.

Things to look for in a fold

Axis The official definition of the axis is the line that moves parallel to itself to generate the fold. In more practical terms, it is the line around which the fold is bent.

Plunge If the axis is not horizontal, it makes an angle to the horizontal called the plunge.

Axial plane This is the plane joining up the axes of the various beds in the fold. It may be vertical in a symmetrical fold, or inclined in an asymmetrical fold.

Competent beds Those that tend to hold their original shape when deformed. They tend to break rather than bend.

Incompetent beds Those that deform when they are folded.

Joints Cracks that open up because of the deformation. These can be strike joints if they are parallel to the axis, or dip joints if they are at right angles to it. Joints may form throughout the rock parallel to the axial plane. Often these tend to fan out,

especially in beds of coarse sandstone.

Dip and Strike These were described on pp. 46–47.

Puckers or parasitic folds These form when very fine beds, such as shale, deform on a small scale as the fold forms.

The symbols are those used on conventional geological mapping.

Below In the field there are a number of features that we can examine in a fold. Most of them can help us to understand the forces that produced the fold in the first place. The orientation of the fold can tell us the direction from which the forces came, and the cracks and joints can show the stresses to which the rocks were subjected.

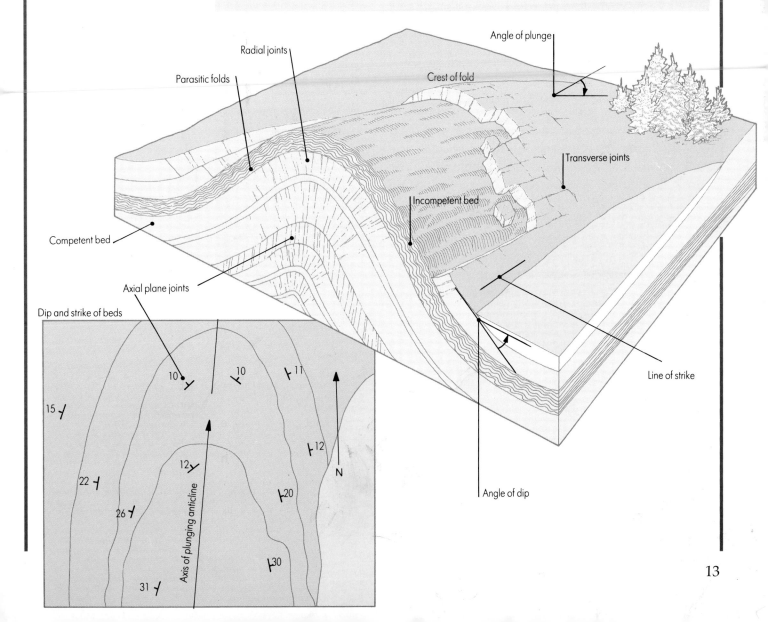

Radial joints

Parasitic folds

Angle of plunge

Crest of fold

Transverse joints

Incompetent bed

Competent bed

Axial plane joints

Dip and strike of beds

Line of strike

Angle of dip

10

10

11

15

12

22

20

12

26

N

30

31

Axis of plunging anticline

Faulted rocks

Sometimes rocks do not bend. Instead they break, and the rock masses move in relation to one another. This action is called faulting. Faults come in many different forms.

A dip-slip fault is produced when the movement is vertical, without any sideways component. The crack or the plane along which the fault moves does not itself need to be vertical, but is usually inclined. In a normal fault, one block has slipped down in relation to the other, down the inclined fault plane. This is produced by tension, as the rocks are pulled apart. A reversed fault or a thrust fault is one in which one block appears to have moved up the fault plane in relation to the other. This is caused by compression.

A strike-slip fault or a lateral fault is one in which the movement is predominantly horizontal. These can be further defined by the movement that has taken place – either a left lateral fault or a right lateral fault depending on which way the opposite block appears to have moved.

More often the fault is an oblique one, in which there have been both horizontal and vertical movements.

When a block moves vertically downward between two faults, the structure is called a graben. If this forms a topographical feature on the surface it is a rift valley. If a block is left upstanding as the rock masses at each side are downfaulted, the result is a horst. A geomorphological feature so produced is called a block mountain.

However, the faults do not always show themselves at the Earth's surface as hills, valleys, cliffs and so on. If the faults are very old, the whole area tends to be eroded so much that no difference in elevation between the faulted blocks can be seen. This may pose difficulties when analyzing faults, particularly in dipping strata. It may not be obvious if a particular fault is a dip-slip fault, a strike-slip fault or an oblique-slip fault. We may have to look for other features, such as the presence of veins or intrusive igneous rocks, to estimate the displacement.

Faults can be very small, with a throw of only a few inches or centimeters. However, because of the huge-scale movements of plate tectonics, some can be thousands of miles or kilometers long. The San Andreas Fault of western North America runs for at least 807 miles (1300 km) and is caused by the relative movements of the Pacific Plate and North American Plate. It is in reality a swarm of right lateral faults, mostly parallel to one another. Movement along it has been in the region of 10 miles (16 km) over the last two million years. It is the movements along faults such as these that cause earthquakes.

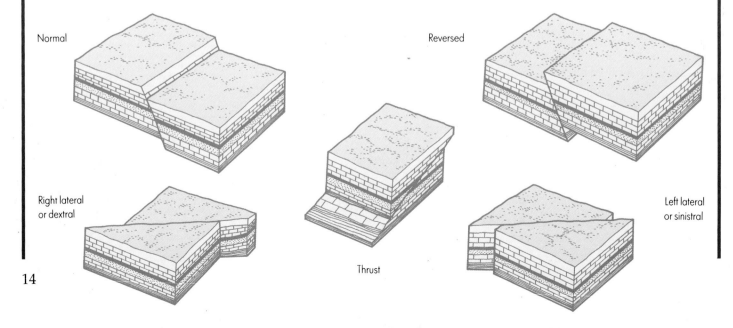

Normal

Reversed

Right lateral or dextral

Left lateral or sinistral

Thrust

Left The complex fracturing of this outcrop in Iran shows all kinds of faults, including normal faults **left**, a reversed fault **bottom center**, and a graben **top center**.

Right and below right As in a fold, we can examine various features associated with a fault in the field, and most of these will give us some idea of the Earth forces that caused the disruption to the rocks – for example, whether the forces were tensional or compressional, and the direction in which they operated.

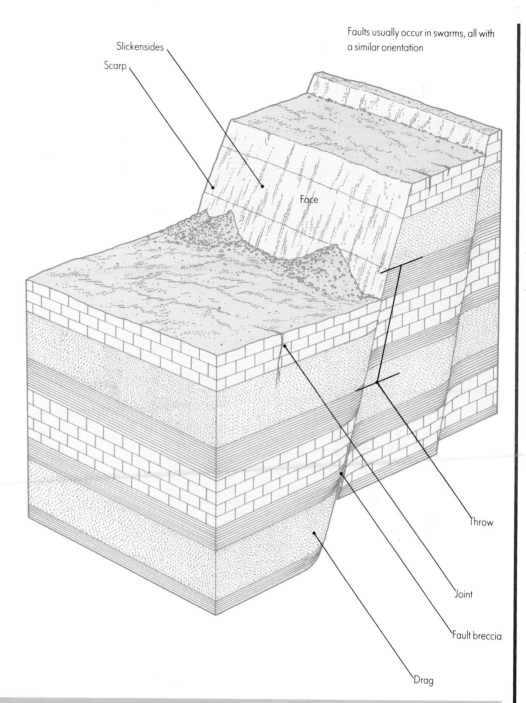

Faults usually occur in swarms, all with a similar orientation

Slickensides

Scarp

Face

Throw

Joint

Fault breccia

Drag

Things to look for in a fault

The fault shown is a normal dip-slip fault.

Throw or offset The distance moved by the fault, only measurable where different beds can be matched up.

Face The surface along which the fault has moved.

Slickensides Polished scratch marks showing where one block has moved across the other.

Scarp The topographic feature produced at the surface if erosion has not worn it all flat.

Fault breccia A mass of rocky material broken and crushed by the movement of the fault. In extreme cases this may form the metamorphic rock mylonite.

Drag Often the beds at each side of the fault are distorted and folded in the direction of the fault movement. This is known as drag.

Joint A break in the rock along which there has been no relative movement is called a joint.

EROSION AND GEO-MORPHOLOGY

The relentless movement of the Earth's surface plates causes landscapes to be uplifted and mountains to be heaved skyward; no sooner is an area of rock raised above sea level than the wind and the rain, the ice and the rivers, the sun and gravity all act to break it down once more. The shape of landscapes (geomorphology) can be seen as the temporary balance between these forces.

Natural decay

Visit a graveyard, preferably an old one. The recent gravestones will be fairly clean, and their inscriptions will be fresh. However, the older ones will be worn and decayed, and the oldest will be almost indecipherable. See which is the oldest date that you can read.

Most of the older monuments will be of the same stone – probably a local stone – and you will see how quickly that stone erodes once it is exposed by looking at the inscribed dates. This tends not to work for more modern gravestones, since they may be sculpted from a wider variety of materials.

If the graveyard consists of monuments made from many different kinds of stone, you will find that some kinds weather more quickly than others. The metamorphic rock marble, for example, decays surprisingly rapidly compared to the sedimentary limestone from which it is derived.

Different climates impose different rates of weathering. Hot damp conditions tend to rot any material quicker than cold dry ones. However, under any conditions, two types of weathering can be distinguished – physical weathering and chemical weathering.

Physical weathering

In the first of these it is the mechanical effects of wind and torrential rain, frost, and animal movements that produce the erosion.

Perhaps the most important factor in higher latitude and altitude rock erosion is frost. Rainwater seeps into pores and cracks in the rock. When this freezes to ice it expands by about nine percent of its volume, forcing open the pores and cracks – in the same way that water pipes become damaged if allowed to freeze in the winter. More water can then seep in and when this freezes even more force is applied. The pressure applied can be about a hundred times greater than the pressure of air in a car tire. Eventually the exposed rock disintegrates into rubble, shattered angular blocks of which lie in long slopes termed scree sweeping down from jagged splintery rock faces.

In hot dry climates the difference in temperature between day and night can have a destructive effect. Rocks expand in the heat and contract in the cold. When this happens to exposed surface layers, they tend to become separated from underlying layers. This is most obvious when the rocks are distinctly bedded, with planes of weakness parallel to the surface. When it happens on massive rocks such as granite, the result is that the rock erodes in curved slabs, a process that is given the technical term exfoliation, or the more descriptive term onion-skin weathering. This action is undoubtedly aided by what is known as pressure release, as the rocks expand after an overburden is eroded away. Chemical weathering may also have a part to play in this complex business.

The real mover in arid landscapes is the wind. The wind can pick up dry particles and hurl them along, blasting them against exposed rocks and

Scree slopes, such as those in the English Lake District **above**, are produced by physical weathering. Water in pores and cracks in the rock expands as it freezes, forcing the rocks apart. Biological erosion takes place as tree roots seek out joints in the rock and then split the rock as they grow, as in this Philippine example **far left**. Onion-skin weathering, where a rock spalls away layer by layer, as here in Tanzania **left**, is caused by both physical and chemical erosion in arid climates.

17

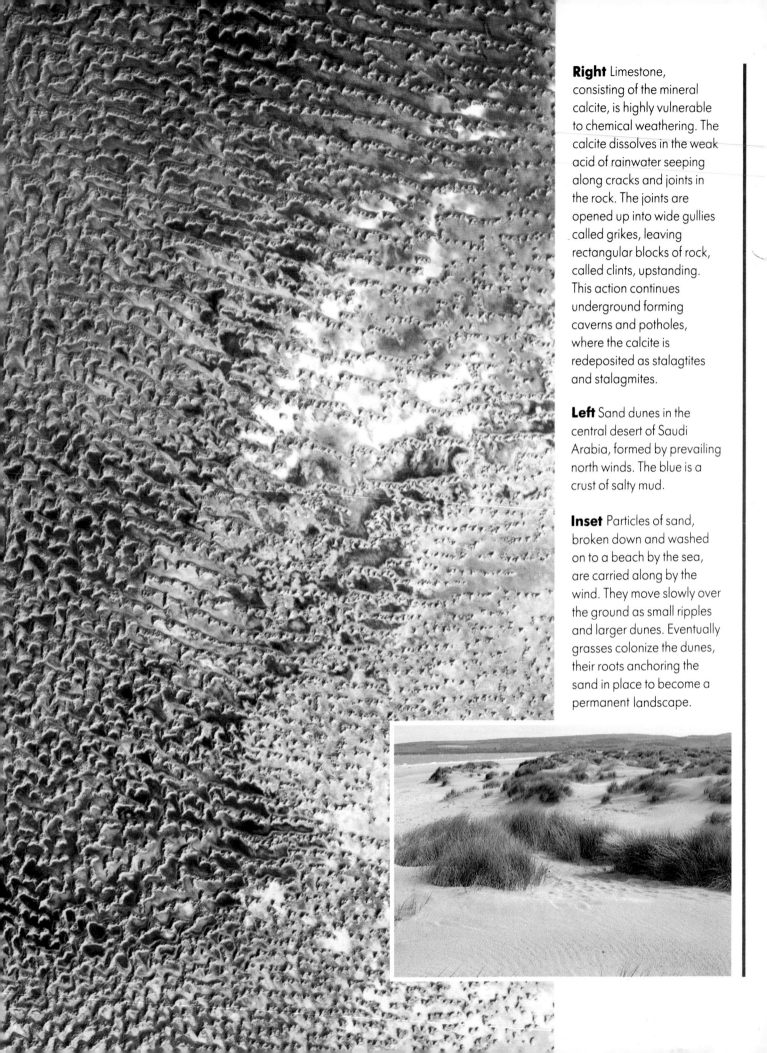

Right Limestone, consisting of the mineral calcite, is highly vulnerable to chemical weathering. The calcite dissolves in the weak acid of rainwater seeping along cracks and joints in the rock. The joints are opened up into wide gullies called grikes, leaving rectangular blocks of rock, called clints, upstanding. This action continues underground forming caverns and potholes, where the calcite is redeposited as stalagtites and stalagmites.

Left Sand dunes in the central desert of Saudi Arabia, formed by prevailing north winds. The blue is a crust of salty mud.

Inset Particles of sand, broken down and washed on to a beach by the sea, are carried along by the wind. They move slowly over the ground as small ripples and larger dunes. Eventually grasses colonize the dunes, their roots anchoring the sand in place to become a permanent landscape.

gradually wearing them down. Most of this action takes place close to the ground where the sand particles are being bounced along. A common result is a rock that looks like a mushroom, with a broad head and a narrow stalk that has been polished away by the sandblasting. Another result is the dreikanter, a stone that has been polished on three sides. A stone lies on the ground. Sand driven by the prevailing wind wears down one side. It becomes unbalanced and so topples over, exposing another side to be polished.

An effect of all this blasting and polishing is that more sand is produced, which adds more force to the sandblasting. Desert sand is moved over the desert floor as slow-motion waves, ie dunes.

A final aspect of physical weathering is the role of living things. Trees growing in soil sink their roots into the bedrock. These roots follow cracks and expand them, splitting the rock open. Certain shellfish can even burrow into rocks, breaking them down.

Nowadays the most potent biological agents of physical erosion are people. Inappropriate farming methods can destroy topsoil. Well-worn footpaths and tracks become incised into the landscape, especially where the native rock is something soft like loess. There is hardly a corner of the globe where human beings have not been a major influence in landscape formation.

Chemical weathering

The gentle rain can often be quite harsh. It may be very acidic, either because it has dissolved acidic industrial gases, or more probably because it has dissolved carbon dioxide from the atmosphere and formed carbonic acid.

Certain minerals are susceptible to attack by this airborne acid, notably feldspar and calcite. Granite consists mostly of quartz, feldspar, and mica. In wet climates the feldspar can react with atmospheric acid and decay into clay minerals. This loosens the other minerals in the rock and they fall out. As a result granite landscapes have china clay quarries, and white beaches of quartz and mica sand by the sea.

Limestone, which consists largely of calcite, is also eroded by acidic rain. The water seeps along joints and cracks, dissolving their sides as it goes, and these cracks are opened up into crevices called grikes, leaving the intervening rocks as

upstanding blocks called clints.

Basic igneous rock such as gabbro is also weathered in this way. The olivine is particularly susceptible, but more to water than to the acid it contains. Water penetrates along joints and attacks all sides at once. The result is that the fresh rock is eroded away. The corners are most vulnerable and become worn off so that the mass becomes a collection of spheres – hence spheroidal weathering.

The chemistry of erosion

The reactions involved in chemical weathering are quite complex, involving the production of soluble substances that are then washed away.

Water (H_2O) dissolves carbon dioxide (CO_2) and becomes carbonic acid (H_2CO_3).

The reaction with feldspar to produce clay minerals –

$6H_2CO_3 + 2KAlSi_3O_8 = Al_2Si_2O_5(OH)_4$ (clay) + $4SiO(OH)_ + K_2CO_3$ (soluble)

The reaction with calcite –

$2H_2CO_3 + 2CaCO_3 = H_2 + 2CaHCO_3$ (soluble)

19

UNDERGROUND LANDSCAPES

The rain falling on the landscape mostly percolates into the ground. It gathers in the saturation zone, where all the pores and crevices of the rock and soil are filled with water. The top of this zone is the water table – an important concept in engineering and drilling wells. Where the water table reaches the surface, as on a slope, the water seeps out in the form of a spring.

In a limestone terrain the situation can be more complex, and more spectacular. Limestone is made of calcite which dissolves away in the carbonic acid of the rain water. On the surface this solution takes place most quickly along the joints and fault planes, opening up crevices and separating the limestone mass into clints. This takes place underground too.

Most erosion follows the bedding planes of the limestone and the joints that tend to cut the bedding plane at right angles. It also takes place along the water table, where the surface of the water may form a stream and flow more or less horizontally. As a result a limestone terrain becomes dissolved into a series of interlocking caverns. From time to time the water table may drop. A stream in a tunnel will then erode deeply into its bed and give a tunnel that is keyhole-shaped in cross-section. If the water table drops suddenly (in geological terms) the stream will begin to erode a new tunnel at the new level and leave the old one as a dry gallery. As the caverns expand, their roofs collapse, filling their floors and opening new spaces above. The collapse may cause the surface to cave in, leaving long gorges along the course of underground rivers, or broad depressions called dolines.

Vertical caves carved out by falling water are called potholes (not to be confused with the potholes that are carved out by swirling stones in a youthful river bed) or sink holes. Surface streams flowing off an area of impermeable rock may suddenly disappear down one of these when it meets limestone.

Some calcite is washed away to sea, but much of it is redeposited in the same area. Groundwater seeping through and hanging as a drop on the cavern roof may deposit its calcite there. Not because the water evaporates away – the humidity of a typical cavern would preclude this – but because the carbon dioxide is lost from the water and it ceases to be acidic enough to hold the

Below and far right
Groundwater sinks into holes and cracks dissolved into limestone 1. At the water table it will flow horizontally, dissolving out a tunnel. Around it other openings will be dissolved along natural bedding planes and cracks in the rock 2. If the water table is lowered, the process is repeated at the lower level, leaving the original tunnel as a dry gallery 3. The ceiling may fall, opening up huge caverns.

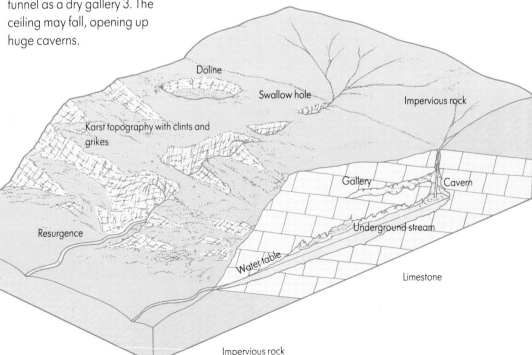

calcite. Accumulation of these calcite deposits builds up stalactites. When a drop hits the cave floor, the calcite is knocked out of it and an accumulation here forms a stalagmite. Different shapes of stalactite and stalagmite develop, each with a descriptive name. Water drawn along a stalagmite or a stalactite by capillary action, for example, will deposit its calcite seemingly at random and produce a twisted stalactite called a helictite.

Calcite is deposited by agitation in the underground stream as well. As an underground stream flows over an irregularity it deposits calcite, which causes a bigger irregularity which deposits more calcite, and so on. The result is a sequence of steps and terraces in the stream bed looking just like a hillside of terraced paddy fields – structures called gours.

When the underground stream finally reaches the surface, it may form a petrifying spring. Here the water can evaporate and deposit its calcite on anything handy. Mosses are sometimes encrusted, as are trinkets left by sightseers.

Calcite is an important mineral in cementing unconsolidated sediment to form a solid rock. A visit to a petrifying spring where the speed of calcite deposition can actually be seen is a memorable demonstration of this.

Above A stream flowing onto a limestone surface may dissolve away a vertical shaft for itself, forming a sinkhole. In the underground caverns and hollows, the dissolved calcite is redeposited on the ceilings and floors in the form of stalactites and stalagmites **below right**.

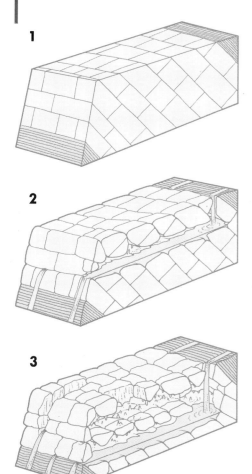

ICE

Ice can be a great rock destroyer, as we have seen , but it can also be a great rock mover and landscape sculptor. In tundra regions, fringing the great ice caps of the colder corners of our globe, the permanently frozen subsoil – the permafrost – has all kinds of influences on the landscape, crazing the surface into huge polygons many yards across, or heaving up vast soil-covered, ice-filled blisters called pingos.

Flowing ice

It is the work of glaciers, those rivers of ice that creep down from the snow-capped mountains, that has the greatest influence on our planet's surface. Snow builds up in a mountain hollow, year after year. Eventually the great weight of the top layers compresses the bottom layers into ice. Under great pressure ice can move like putty and the whole mass creeps downhill. As it goes, its great weight grinds out the floor and sides of its valley, and carries the resulting debris along. Valley walls are undercut and avalanches bring more debris down on to the icy surface. A glacier is like a huge conveyor belt for rocks and stones.

More impressive are the ice caps – vast masses of ice that sit over the Earth's poles or on ice-bound continents, and creep outward as more snow falls in the center.

Evidence of ice past

This may not seem to have much relevance to the landscape of the more temperate parts of the world. However, we have just seen the back of the Great Ice Age that has affected the world for the last two million years. Much of North America, Europe, and Asia were covered in ice sheets, and the glaciers extended down from the mountain valleys in other parts of the world. Everywhere in these areas we see landforms that have been sculpted by the ice masses.

Below left and right The great weight of a glacier grinds down the floor and sides of its valley, carrying along the debris it has torn out. When the glacier has eventually melted, the valley will have a characteristic U-shape. The floor may consist of smooth polished rock, and the material carried along – the moraine – will be deposited elsewhere, either as formless sheets of boulder clay, or as hummocks called drumlins. The path of a former stream under the ice may be marked by a ridge called an esker.

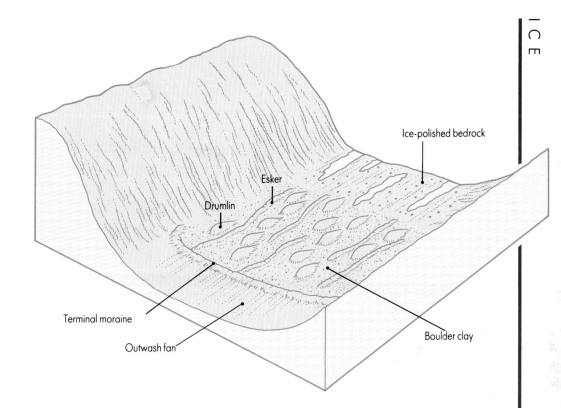

Ice-polished bedrock

Esker

Drumlin

Terminal moraine

Outwash fan

Boulder clay

The deepened and broadened valleys have taken on a distinctive U-shape, with their tributary valleys left hanging halfway up the side walls. When submerged by the sea, these form fjords. Bare rock faces have been gouged with deep scratches called striations. Exposed outcrops have been polished and striated on their upstream side, and shattered and pulled away on the downstream side, leaving the outcrop as a structure called a *roche moutonneé*.

The redistributed debris
Geologists give it the term moraine. It lies in the lowlands where the glaciers finally melted. Huge boulders, coarse rubble, and fine clay particles are all deposited together when the ice melts to form boulder clay. This can be a simple layer over the landscape, or it may form mounds called drumlins several hundred yards or meters long and orientated in the direction of the original ice flow. Sometimes a long winding structure forms, like a sinuous railroad embankment, produced where a stream in a tunnel within the glacier carried rubble along and deposited it at the glacier's snout. This structure is termed an esker. Where the glacier melted back in stages, the moraine lies in curved ridges, each ridge marking the former position of the glacier's snout.

As a moraine contains debris that has been lifted and carried along by the glacier, it can be used to detect the direction from which the glacier traveled. Erratic blocks are particularly useful for this. These are very large boulders that have been shifted by a glacier and dumped somewhere where the geology is entirely different. For example, the erratic blocks found on the east coast of England are composed of rocks found in the Norwegian highlands.

Something to do

Find an outcrop of boulder clay. (Local geological excursion guides will help you find such a place.) Gather a sample of it. Do a rough analysis of the size of particles – dig out boulders and cobbles and put them on one side, put pebbles on another, regard the clay groundmass as the finest material. You will find that they have been all mixed up together. A glacier does not discriminate the size of material it carries. It is strong enough to carry the heaviest, yet it can grind things down to the finest grade. Then, when it melts, it dumps everything haphazardly.

COASTAL EROSION

The sea with its churning currents and pounding waves is, not surprisingly, a very powerful erosional agent.

The physical pressure of walls of water thumping against exposed rock compresses the air in pores and cracks in the rock, forcing it to expand explosively as soon as the pressure is released. This pressure is on average nearly 2500 pounds per square foot (10 tonnes per square meter) but during a storm it can be five times as great. Soft cliffs can be worn back at a rate of one yard or meter per year by this hydraulic action.

Boulders and pebbles picked up from the sea bed are hurled at cliff faces, smashing off more fragments. This process is known as corrasion. The boulders and pebbles themselves are smashed and ground down in the process known as attrition.

There is also a chemical reaction between the salts in the seawater and the minerals of some rocks, and a biological reaction involving grazing seasnails and certain kinds of rock-dissolving bacteria. All these effects combine to erode the sea cliffs.

The crumbling headlands

The erosional effects tend to be concentrated on headlands. Waves attack along a front, defined by the direction of the wind and the shape of the sea bed. As waves approach a headland, they slow down as they meet the shallow water near the headland itself, but continue at the same speed at

In a cliff eroded by the sea, the softer beds will erode first, leaving the harder beds jutting out **top**. When a sea cave forms, the waves funneling into it will build up a tremendous air pressure, forcing the rocks apart. Any crack forced through to the outside will produce a blast of air and water every time a wave crashes into the cave below. This produces a blowhole **left**. Headlands are eroded from both sides. The caves and blowholes eroded along the softer rocks and weaker zones may meet in the middle of the headland and form a tunnel or a natural arch. Eventually the roof of the arch will fall, leaving the seaward portion standing as a seastack **below**

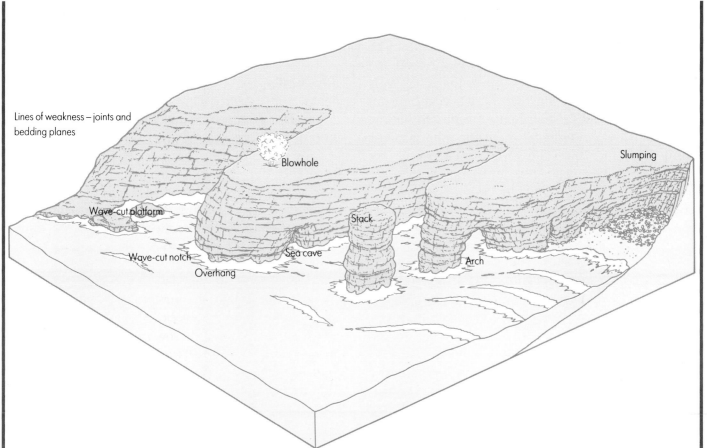

Lines of weakness – joints and bedding planes

Blowhole

Slumping

Wave-cut platform

Stack

Wave-cut notch

Sea cave

Arch

Overhang

each side. As a result the wave front curves around and attacks both flanks of the headland. Cracks are widened into sea caves, and these are themselves widened by the explosive effect of the hydraulic pressure on the trapped air. Occasionally a hole is blown through the roof, and the incoming wave has a piston effect, blasting air and spray out as a blowhole. Caves on opposite sides of a headland can meet each other, producing a tunnel or a natural arch. Eventually, as the arch is worn away, the lintel falls, leaving the offshore part of the headland isolated. The result is a sea stack, which is itself eventually demolished. Coastlines are continually eroded back by such repeated demolition of headlands.

Wave erosion is confined to the areas that waves can reach. When a sloping coastline is attacked, the waves erode the few yards or meters close to sea level. As the coast is worn back, this cuts a notch which can be quite an even and graceful curve in homogeneous rock. The resulting overhang eventually collapses into the sea. The debris is soon cleared away by current and wave action and the undercutting continues. Erosion takes place by the retreat of the cliff so

formed. The shape of the cliff is determined largely by its geology. Soft material such as sand or clay forms a sloping crumbling cliff, while something with a relatively even composition and texture forms a fairly smooth vertical surface. Strongly bedded or deeply jointed rocks erode irregularly, erosion being swiftest along the planes of weakness.

Coastal patterns

On a wider scale, the regional geology determines the nature of the coastline. Strata that run parallel to the sea produce a so-called Pacific type coastline with inlets that cut through the ridges and spread out in broad inlets along the softer rock – as in San Francisco Bay – and elongated islands and reefs parallel to the coast. On the other hand, strata that run straight out to sea produce a deeply indented coastline, with the hard rocks forming long headlands and the soft eroding to long bays. Southwestern Ireland is a magnificent example, and the result is called an Atlantic type coastline. The constant opening up of fresh cliff faces along an area of coastal erosion makes such places ideal prospecting sites.

COASTAL ACCRETION

The waves can destroy. They can also build. The boulders, cobbles, and pebbles washed off the headlands and the cliffs, and the sands and gravels ground down from the bigger fragments, are all washed about and redistributed, eventually ending up deposited someplace where the land is being built up rather than destroyed. Such places are seen as beaches, sand spits, and sand bars.

Beaches on the march

Two important concepts in this are longshore drift and beach drift. The first is caused by currents that sweep along the coastline, moving material parallel to the shore. The second is caused by the waves that usually strike the shore at an angle. As they do so, any pebbles or sand grains that they carry are washed diagonally up the beach. As the water recedes after every wave it pours straight back down the slope of the beach, carrying the debris with it. The next surge of the wave carries the fragments diagonally up once more, and then straight back down. As a result, each piece of beach material follows a zigzag route along the beach. Coastal communities often fear that this action will take away their beaches and so barriers are installed, projecting into the sea at right angles of the coast. These are called groynes, and trap the beach sediment on one side. From the air the resulting beach has a distinctive saw-toothed pattern.

Bars and spits

Beach drifting carries the sand along the coastline until it reaches an opening or a river mouth. There it continues in its journey and builds out a tongue of sand called a spit. The wave front, like that at a headland, curves around the end of the spit and deposits more sediment on the back of the tip. As a result, a typical sand spit has a hooked end which appears to curve upstream. Such a spit rarely goes all the way across a river mouth, since the current tends to carry much of the sediment away and leave an opening. However, the presence and the continual buildup of a spit may move a river mouth along the coast in the direction of the prevailing wave fronts, so that the river now reaches the sea many miles or kilometers away from its original mouth. A good example of this is the River Alde in eastern England. A sand spit called Orford Ness, built up by the currents and waves of the North Sea, has moved its mouth about 5 miles (8 km) south of its original site.

When a spit is built up right across the mouth of an inlet the result is a sand bar, cutting off an area of water to form a lagoon. Many of these are seen around the south coast of the Baltic Sea. The region of the Baltic is slowly rising, and so the sea is constantly changing its shape, and the deposition pattern is changing with it. A sand spit often reaches out to an island, linking it to the mainland. The resulting landscape feature is called a tombolo – an Italian name owing to the fact that many of them exist along the west coast of Italy.

Left A combination of sea currents and waves carries sand along a shoreline. To prevent beaches from being washed away, the authorities often build barriers, groynes, running out to sea. The sand builds up on the upstream side, but continues to be washed away from the downstream side, producing a zigzag beach pattern.

Right Waves usually approach a beach at an angle. Sand particles are washed up the beach at that angle. When the wave recedes, the water and the sand particles wash directly down the slope. The next wave washes them up at an angle again. As a result, sand moves along a beach with the constant wash of the waves.

Left The moving sand will build out beyond the end of its beach as a sand spit. If this spit continues right across an opening, cutting off a lagoon, it is called a sand bar. Sometimes a bar will connect an island to the mainland, such as here in the Indian Ocean. The resulting feature is called a tombolo.

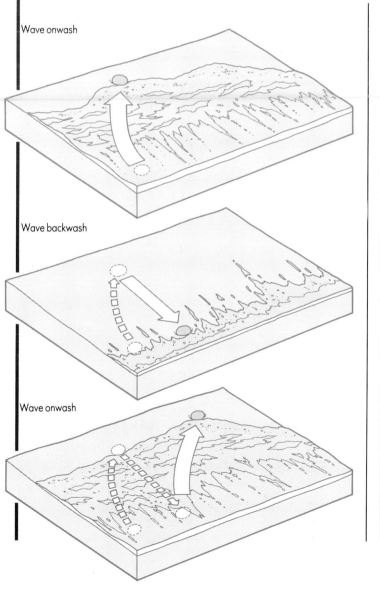

Wave onwash

Wave backwash

Wave onwash

A conflict of currents

Beach drift moving in from two different directions may bring sediment that piles up in a low triangular headland consisting largely of gravel ridges. One of the best examples is Cape Canaveral in Florida, where gravel has been piled up by conflicting eddies from the Gulf Stream. Sand and other light materials brought up by the waves may then be picked up and carried along by the wind. This is the origin of the sand dunes that often back up exposed ocean beaches.

Something to do

Go to the beach in the summer. Take a photograph of the beach from a particular point. Take samples of the beach material – sand, gravel, or whatever – at that time. Go back to the same spot in the winter. Take another photograph from exactly the same position, and gather another sample of beach material. Then do the same thing the following summer.

The changes in beach material will show the different energies of waves – coarse gravel is shifted by much fiercer waves than fine sand – and the photographs will show marked changes brought about in a very short time.

FIELD WORK TECHNIQUE

As well as knowing what to look for, it is essential to know how to go about finding it, and recognizing it when we see it.

Right In a landscape of extrusive igneous rocks, the soil underfoot is formed from decaying lava – either basaltic or andesitic. Old lava flows may be obvious in the outcropping rocks. The horizon will consist of the conical peaks of old volcanoes. A landscape of intrusive igneous rocks, however, may be similar to that produced by metamorphic rocks.

TECHNIQUES FOR IGNEOUS ROCKS

In a region of igneous rocks, it is a good idea to look first for the the contact between the igneous rock and the original rock. Finding it will be a great help to the mapping of the area. If the boundary between the igneous and the native rocks is well defined, note its strike and dip, determine whether it cuts across the "grain" of the original rocks or is concordant with it, note whether it is a sharp boundary or diffuse, see what effect it has on the wall rocks, and observe any metamorphism that has taken place.

Structures and shapes
From these observations you should be able to determine whether the rock is in the structure of a batholith, a dike or a sill, or a lava flow.

Now look for any cooling features. These would include the columnar jointing we would expect to see in a quickly-cooled basalt flow, or a chilled margin in which the mineral crystals close to the contact with the native rock are more finely grained than the rest of the mass, or extensive veins that filled with minerals at a late stage of a slow cooling.

Crystals and inclusions

Look for vesicles – bubbles of gas like those trapped near the top of a basaltic lava flow. Look for amygdales – exactly the same but filled with mineral. This would help to distinguish whether a lava flow was recent, with vesicles, or old, in which case there would have been time for the vesicles to be filled with minerals deposited by groundwater. Determine the mineral content of the amygdales – usually calcite or quartz.

See if there are any flow structures within the

igneous mass, such as concentrations of crystals toward the center of the structure. Note any signs of layering, in which some minerals may have solidified and settled while the bulk of the mass was still liquid. Note the presence of phenocrysts – crystals that are much larger than those in the rest of the mass. These would suggest that the igneous mass began to cool slowly and then finished cooling much more swiftly.

Look for xenoliths – chunks of the original rock that were caught up in liquid flow and have become embedded in the final igneous rock. These will be metamorphosed. Note the effects of metamorphism, both on the xenoliths and on the native rock round about.

Note if there is only one phase of igneous activity, or if there are several – with dikes cutting across sills. Note the orientation of all structural features, such as joints, and try to discern a pattern later.

What is it made of?

When you take a sample, number it and enter the observation in your notebook or map. On the spot you can note the size and shape of the specimen – important if the specimen is a volcanic bomb or a xenolith – the color and density, giving a rough guide to the mineralogy, and the texture and grain size. Identify as many of the constituent minerals as possible, using the hand lens and your other field kit such as your hardness points and your streak plate. You should have enough information by now to give the rock sample a provisional name. Then pack it up safely so that you can study it at leisure when you get back home or to the laboratory.

TECHNIQUES FOR SEDIMENTARY ROCKS

Take a walk up a stream bed. Gather up the pebbles that interest you. Chip away at a fossil exposed in the bank. Pry a well-formed crystal from a vein. You are now a rockhound! You are not being a geologist.

Patient and methodical field work is needed if your experience and findings are to have a lasting value and enjoyment. Develop a routine.

Before beginning your trip, take a note of the

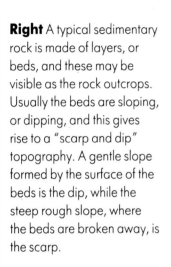

Right A typical sedimentary rock is made of layers, or beds, and these may be visible as the rock outcrops. Usually the beds are sloping, or dipping, and this gives rise to a "scarp and dip" topography. A gentle slope formed by the surface of the beds is the dip, while the steep rough slope, where the beds are broken away, is the scarp.

date in your field notebook, and make some general remarks about the nature of the work you are about to undertake. By reading your map and looking at the area from a distance you will see the most likely places for outcrops – disused quarries, stream gullies, highway excavations, and so on. You will be able to work out a makeshift itinerary.

At each outcrop, take a note of its position and mark it on your map. If you are in open country, far from any mapped feature, take cross-bearings from recognizable landmarks or from your starting point. Note the kind of outcrop – an isolated exposure, a cliff face, a stream section, or whatever. If it is interesting enough, sketch it in your notebook, recording the scale of the sketch and the direction from which it is viewed.

Measurement of the beds
In a sedimentary rock, measure the dip and the strike by using the clinometer and a compass. Enter the readings on your map, using the conventional symbols. Beware of the apparent dip. It may be that an exposure in a vertical sea cliff face shows a bed to be dipping, but the orientation of the cliff face may not be parallel to the dip, so the dip reading will be wrong. You must find a three-dimensional exposure, possibly in the wave-cut platform at the base of the cliff, in

order to find the strike and the direction of true dip. If you cannot do this, then the apparent dip should be noted and marked as such. The dip may be irregular, as on a surface showing current bedding or ripple marks, in which case you must make several measurements over as large an area as possible, and take an average.

Note also the bed's thickness. Always measure the thickness at right angles to the dip.

The structures

If the outcrop is of a complex nature – as in two sequences of rocks separated by an unconformity – study it systematically in its logical sequence. Describe the lower beds first. Then deal with the nature of the unconformity, noting whether or not the first series of beds is eroded irregularly with a conglomerate on top (as would have happened when the sea flooded the land) or planed flat (as would be formed at the bottom of the sea). Then study the overlying beds.

In any sequence, study the rocks in their order of deposition, starting at the bottom and working upward. Make a rough identification of the fossils you find, selecting the more interesting ones for careful examination later.

Note the post-depositional structures – the folding and the faulting. Record the orientations of fold axes, faults, and joints. Do as many as you can and try to work out a pattern for them later.

Every sample you take must be labeled immediately. Attach a gummed label with a serial number that you note in your field notebook or on your map. Wrap it carefully and pack it for safe transportation back.

TECHNIQUES FOR METAMORPHIC ROCKS AND DRIFT

Thermal metamorphic rocks are usually studied at the same time as the igneous intrusion that metamorphosed them. Regional metamorphic rocks, on the other hand, tend to be the subject of separate expeditions and studies.

Looking at regional structure

At each outcrop observe the texture, the banding, the foliation, and the schistosity. Note the orienta-

Which way up?

Sometimes in highly contorted terrain it is difficult to see which way up the beds should be. The concept of younging comes into play. Look for features that could only have been deposited one way up – graded bedding has the coarsest material at the bottom, current bedding is concave upward, as are sole marks and tool marks.

31

tion and inclination of these. If the original rock has been sedimentary, see if there is any sign of the original bedding, and note the dip and strike of this. See also if there are the remains of any fossils or other sedimentary features, and note the extent of their deformation.

Regional metamorphic rocks tend to occur in mountainous areas, and so such an expedition may take you to remote places. You should bear this in mind when collecting specimens. A small specimen should be good enough for a fine-grained rock, but if you get back and find the small specimen inadequate it will probably be a long hike back to get another one. As usual, trim your specimen to show fresh faces, but if the weathered face helps to show up the texture then preserve this as well.

When noting the texture and structure of the rock, see if the crystals are of the same size, or if some are larger than the rest.

The loose stuff

You are unlikely to find that the rocks outcrop over the whole of your area of study. Most of the area will be covered with soil, scree slopes, flood deposits, and other natural material. This is referred to as drift on geological maps, as opposed to the underlying geology which is termed solid. You should become familiar with the features of drift, and how they relate to the solid rocks beneath. Look at the kinds of stones thrown up in rabbit holes and other workings, note any change of vegetation, see if a slope alters its angle – possibly indicating a bed of harder rock.

The study of drift is itself interesting. You will soon be able to distinguish the drift that forms *in situ* from that which has been deposited by other means. If the loose material contains fragments of the underlying rock, then it is safe to assume that it it is a soil formed from the decay of the rocks in that place. Boulder clay, on the other hand, is a jumbled mixture of all sorts of rocks brought in from other areas by ice. This can be something of a headache since it may be dozens of yards or meters thick and effectively isolate the geologist from any solid native rock.

Above Metamorphic rocks, particularly regional metamorphic rocks, tend to be found in the deep interiors of mountain chains, since they are formed by the mountain-building process. In very ancient shield areas, however, the Precambrian mountains have been worn flat, and the result is a low rounded topography.

Blasted geology!

In igneous rocks a texture in which large crystals are scattered through a fine groundmass is called porphyritic. In metamorphic rocks it is called *porphyroblastic*. The prefix "blast-" is one that geologists often use in the study of metamorphic rocks. It means the metamorphosed remains of something else. Hence we get poikiloblastic – a texture in which a fine mass of new minerals forms around the original minerals, and blastopsammite – a piece of sandstone embedded in a metamorphosed conglomerate. Porphyroblastic, however, refers to the new crystals that have grown with the metamorphism, and should not be confused with *blastoporphoritic* in which we see the remains of a porphoritic structure that was present in the original rock.

Confused? Don't worry. Familiarity with specialist terms comes with experience.

GRANITE

The proportions of the chemical components of the continental crust are such that, if they were to be melted down, mixed thoroughly, and slowly cooled, the result would be granite.

Mineralogy

It consists largely of feldspar, quartz, mica, and a small quantity of iron ore.

Landscape and structures

Granite landscapes are usually hills or moorlands. Granite forms in batholiths, deep within mountain chains, and so granite landscapes usually occur where very ancient mountains have been eroded away, for example in the Appalachians or the western peninsula of England. Outcrops also occur where rivers have eroded deeply into mountainous areas, as in the Grand Canyon.

In humid climates the feldspar in the granite tends to decay along joints and cracks, breaking any outcrop into rounded blocks and producing castle-like structures called tors, particularly on moors and along coasts. Take a note of the orientation of these cracks. They may give a clue to the pressures that have affected the region since the granite was emplaced. The feldspar decomposes to produce china clay (kaolin), and so granite moors are often characterized by the white spoil-heaps from china-clay quarries. The decayed feldspar loosens the quartz and mica from the rock and this is washed away, producing dazzlingly white beaches by granite landmasses. Drainage is poor through granite, so bogs tend to form. Take waterproof footgear when looking at granite terrain.

In arid climates most weathering is on the surface rather than along joints. Onion-skin weathering and sand-blasting produce rounded hills called inselbergs or kopjes, such as those that dot the Serengeti wildlife park in Tanzania.

If you are lucky you may find inclusions – chunks of the surrounding rock that were engulfed by the granite when it formed. These will be metamorphosed beyond recognition. You may even see the contact between the batholith and the country rock, and find more metamorphism. The country rock will probably be full of veins, as may the edge of the granite itself, where hot fluids filled cracks as the igneous mass finally cooled. These veins will be made of large crystals of quartz, and may contain large crystals of other minerals as well. The extremely coarse rocks formed in veins are often called pegmatites.

Right Because of the feldspar content, granites are subject to chemical weathering in moist climates. Joints are eroded and the intervening masses are left as rectangular blocks reminiscent of massive masonry. This example is at England's Land's End.

Hand specimen The surface of a granite outcrop is invariably weathered, and so it is necessary to break it open with a hammer to see a fresh face. It is a good idea, however, to retain a weathered face – it may help to show up the texture. There is no internal structure or planes of weakness, and so it will break irregularly. The grain is usually so coarse that you can see the individual mineral crystals –

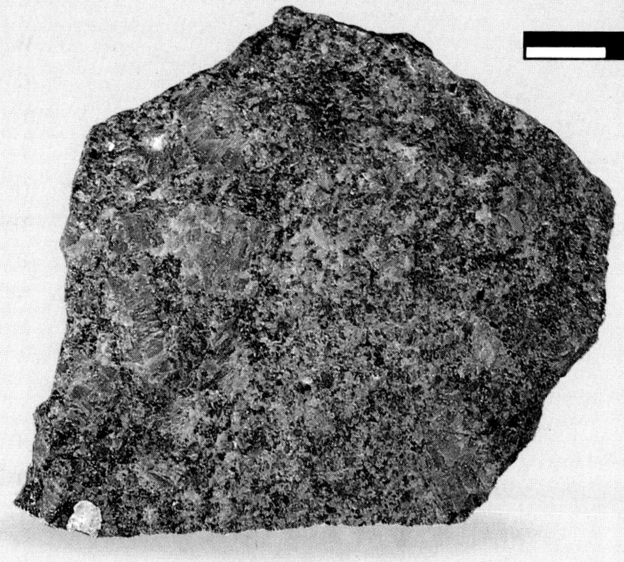

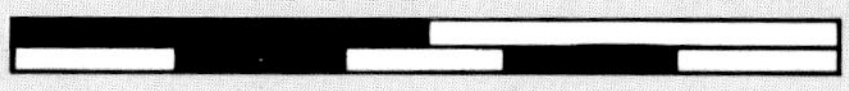
inches
centimeters

the glassy quartz, the milky feldspar, and the dark but sparkling mica. The iron ore will be too small to see.

Microscopic specimen Through the crossed polars of the microscope the most obvious crystals are those of the feldspar. They will usually be twinned, each half of the twin showing a different extinction angle and fading from white to black through shades of gray. The shapeless pieces of quartz

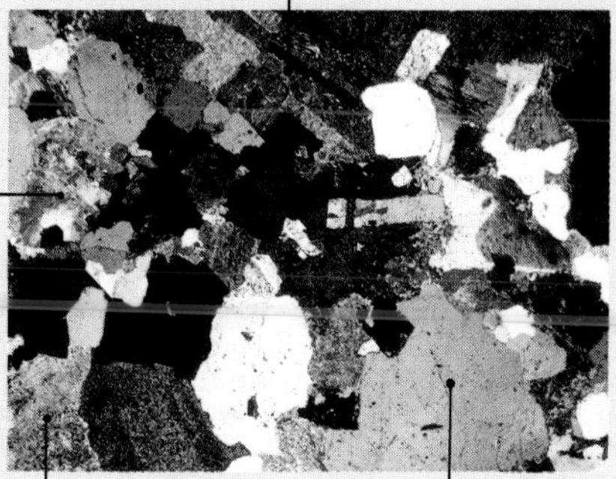
Twinned feldspar with multiple twins
Mica with bright interference colors
Quartz
Untwinned feldspar

are somewhat dull and featureless. The mica will show a range of colors and will have irregular shapes. The iron ore magnetite will be present as tiny grains and will be seen best through a single polarized filter (the polarizer) as opaque fragments amid the general transparency.

Varieties The chemical nature of the feldspars will alter the appearance of a granite outcrop. If the feldspar is rich in potassium it tends to be white in color. The white feldspar and quartz contrast with the black of the mica to give a speckled appearance and an overall gray color. Sodium-rich and calcium-rich feldspars are pink and impart an overall pink color to the rock.

A porphyritic texture is sometimes in evidence, in which the feldspar crystals are so much larger than the others. The very large crystals in a porphyritic texture are called phenocrysts.

The large crystals give granite an attractive appearance, which is why it is often used for building and ornaments.

Similar rocks Syenite is fairly similar in its occurrence and appearance although much less abundant. It is a coarse-grained intrusive rock of intermediate composition – having no quartz but some of the magnesium-iron silicates such as amphibole and pyroxene. The resulting rock has a slightly darker color. The coarse metamorphic rock gneiss has a similar grain size and mineralogy to granite, but it can usually be distinguished by the fact that the minerals form in discrete bands.

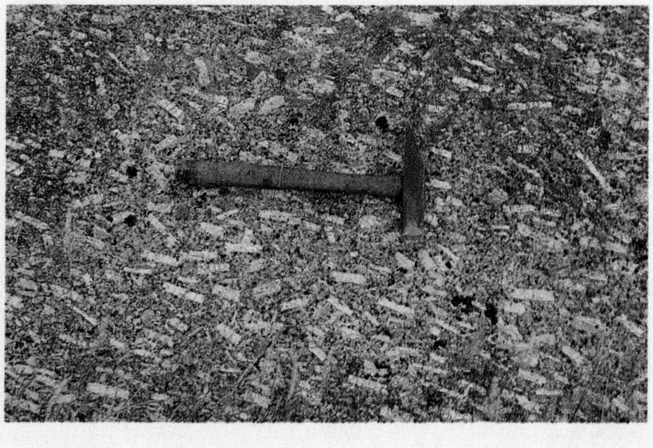

Coarse porphyritic granite

LIMESTONE

Limestone is a sedimentary rock, usually biogenic or chemical in origin. It forms in the shallow waters of shelf seas, and so it tends to cover very large areas.

Mineralogy

Limestone is, basically, a rock made of calcite. However, being a sedimentary rock, it may be mixed in with other minerals depending on how clear the water was when it formed. Dolomite – magnesium carbonate – may be mixed in with it, and in some cases may form the major proportion. Sandy and shaly limestones are common, and it becomes difficult to classify the various grades. As a rule, any rock with more than 50 percent carbonate minerals is classified as a limestone.

Landscape and structures

A limestone terrain is dry. When the limestone is massive – when it comes in thick beds rather than thin slabs interbedded with other rocks – it forms arid upland plateaus. Streams vanish from the surface, dissolving limestone and forming underground caverns. The weathering features called clints and grikes are common, as are collapse features such as gorges and dolines.

Ancient limestone landscapes may have been buried by later sediments, and the erosional features will be fossilized. The rubble from collapsed cave roofs will be cemented together by redistributed calcite and preserved as collapse breccia. Sometimes this preserves the skeletons of animals that lived there when the caves existed. Carboniferous limestone in southwestern England was exposed in Triassic times and its crevices contain the fossils of Triassic reptiles. The same Carboniferous limestone in Belgium formed a ridge in Cretaceous times and Cretaceous dinosaur skeletons have been found in a gorge there.

Where underground streams reach the surface again there may be deposits of tufa.

An outcrop of limestone in an industrial area may be marked by a line of cement factories.

The rugged waterless nature of a limestone landscape is well-known and is due to the chemical weathering of the chief component calcite. Clints and grikes form on flat-lying limestone beds **above** forming a limestone pavement and giving a topography known as a "karst" landscape, named for the area in Yugoslavia. Rivers cut deep steep-sided gorges, by vertical erosion or by collapse of caverns and underground waterways. The Cévennes region of central France **right** has fine examples, such as the Gorges du Tarn and the Gorge de la Jonte.

Hand specimen

Depending on the type of limestone, the hand specimen may be a mass of fossils or it may be an even-grained, pale-colored rock.

When a biological limestone is weathered, it may show the constituent fossils in high relief.

A variety of the chemical limestone called oolite consists of tiny spherical particles about 1/16 in (1 mm) across, called ooliths. In a coarser variety, pisolite, the grains are pea-sized. These have formed as calcite precipitated on fragments of sand or shell, and then rolled about on the sea floor, building up like snowballs.

In the hand specimen you can distinguish between calcite and dolomite by using acid (vinegar will do). Calcite fizzes and bubbles, but dolomite does not react.

Varieties There are many types of limestone. The shelly limestones are usually classified by the kinds of fossils they contain, for example gastropod limestone, crinoidal

Oolitic limestone

inches

centimeters

Shelly limestone

limestone, or coral limestone. Many of these take a good polish, revealing light fossils contrasting with a dark matrix, so are used in building. They are often misleadingly called marbles by stoneworkers; for example, Purbeck marble (a Jurassic limestone with gastropods) and Forsterly marble (a Carboniferous limestone with corals).

Limestone conglomerate consists of small pieces of preexisting limestone, called by the mineralogists intraclasts, cemented together.

There is also a type of limestone that is made up of calcite pellets – similar to ooliths but with no internal structure.

The nature of the cementing groundmass is important. Those cemented together with coarse crystals are called sparites, and those with very fine crystals micrites.

Microscopic specimen

Fragments of the fossil content are usually very recognizable, with the cementing calcite visible as a regular mosaic around them. Sometimes the cementing calcite is grown from an existing calcite fragment and you can see the shape of the original as a ghost in a larger calcite crystal.

Photomicrograph of shelly limestone

In an oolite, the concentric shapes of the individual ooliths are very visible, again cemented together by a calcite mosaic.

CHALK

Chalk is a particularly pure type of biogenic limestone. It formed in extensive massive beds on the floors of broad shallow continental seas at the end of the Cretaceous period.

Mineralogy

Chalk consists almost entirely of calcite, in one form or another. It can be 98 percent pure. It consists of the calcite shells of microscopic marine algae which may or may not be filled with crystaline calcite. As a rule the chalk contains no land-derived sediments whatever, but older beds of chalk may contain some mud particles, and when these become so great that the purity of the calcite drops to about 80 percent the rock becomes chalk marl.

Landscape and structures

A chalk landscape is quite distinctive, forming the rolling downland that is so characteristic of southeast England and northeastern France.

Chalk usually forms grassland as trees do not grow well on it. Beeches are the main trees found, and these usually form discrete thickets and woods. As with other types of limestone terrain, there are few surface streams. However, broad, gently undulating dry valleys abound; these may have been formed during the Ice Age when the groundwater was frozen.

At the sea it forms spectacular white cliffs, such as the famous White Cliffs of Dover. The regular texture means that the cliffs are vertical and straight, and tend to be eroded back evenly, producing a straight coastline.

Silica, which may have been present in the original sediments, collects in distinct levels, as irregular bands of flint lumps, or as beds of chert.

The startlingly white appearance of the naked rock contrasts strongly with any vegetation cover. Pits from which chalk has been excavated are visible from a long way off. Often this is exploited as an art form and shapes such as horses and giants are cut into chalk hillsides by removal of the turf.

Chalk downland is waterless, rainwater seeping through the porous rock to form streams. Soil-creep – the movement of soil down a steep slope – is common on the sides of the dry valleys, forming horizontal ridges called terracettes **below**. Where chalk downland is eroded, in quarries or by the sea, the startlingly white nature of the rock is very marked, as here **right** in Sussex, southern England.

Hand specimen The rock breaks off in irregular dusty pieces as there are no internal structures or zones of weakness. Fossils are so completely encased that they cannot be removed. Any break cuts clean across the fossil. The fossils are usually formed by silica replacement, and if there are any veins present in the rock these will contain silica too. Chalk is so fine-grained that the constituent particles are impossible to see, either with the naked eye or with a hand lens. A grayish tinge may be due to the presence of mud particles in the original sediment. A greenish tinge may be imparted by the iron silicate mineral glauconite, but only in impure chalks.

Varieties Chalk is so pure that the slightest impurity can impart a characteristic color and give it a name. White

chalk is the purest. Gray chalk has fine mud or clay particles. Red chalk contains iron minerals.

Chalk forming on the bottom of the sea may be affected by bottom currents, and may be broken up and redeposited. The broken pieces are then recemented together and may be mixed with nodules of other minerals. The resulting rock is called chalk rock and can be met as distinct beds in chalk sequences.

Microscopic specimen The grain of chalk is so fine that even microscopic investigation can be of little value. Indeed it was only with the invention of the electron microscope in 1932 that it was possible to identify the types of minute shells that formed the bulk of the rock.

SANDSTONE

Sandstone is a clastic sedimentary rock, with a grain size of between 0.0002 in and 0.02 in (0.02 mm and 2 mm). Anything bigger would be a conglomerate or a breccia, anything smaller would be a siltstone, shale, mudstone, or clay. Various types form in deserts, in rivers, and on sea beds.

Mineralogy

The mineralogy of sandstone depends on the rock from which the original sediment weathered, and also on the conditions of deposition of the sediment. Usually it is the most robust minerals that survive as sand grains, and that generally means quartz. Other minerals from the parent rock may also be present if the grains have not traveled far before deposition. Cementing material can be calcite, iron oxide, or more quartz.

Landscape and structures

If the sandstone is derived from desert sands, it will form a massive bed covering a very large area. Dune bedding will be present. The rock will probably have a reddish tinge due to iron oxide that formed when the original sand was exposed to the atmosphere.

River sandstone will be more finely bedded, and will probably be interbedded with other rocks such as shale or mudstone. It is unlikely to be pure and the impurities may make it shaly sandstone or limy sandstone. Current bedding may be present, as may slump bedding. It will not have the reddish hue of desert sandstone. If the cementing material is iron ore, it will be brown; if it is calcite, it will be gray. It may be leached white and full of root fragments, in which case it formed a sandbank above the water surface and had plants growing in it. Watch out for washout structures. These represent the channels of contemporary streams that cut through a sandbank and then filled up with their own sediment. They show as trough-shaped structures filled with sandstone that has a distinctively different bedding from the surrounding rock.

Sandstone formed in shallow seas may be very similar to that formed in rivers. In this case ripple marks will be more common than current bed-

Left Massive sandstone – consisting of thick beds with few bedding planes – will erode into sheer bluffs and towering crags, particularly when exposed to wind erosion, such as here in Utah.

Above Sandstone is a porous rock and holds water very well. In well-watered regions, such as France, a sandstone landscape is able to support a prolific growth of vegetation.

ding. There may be sedimentary dikes and sedimentary volcanoes – self-contradictory terms that describe what happens when a quicksand squirts up through a more rigid layer that has been deposited on top. These may be associated with slump bedding.

Sandstones formed in deep seas are quite different. They may be very coarse and jumbled, or may show graded bedding, depending on the state of the sea-bottom currents that formed them.

When studying sandstones in the field it is important to note the orientation of the strike and the angle of dip. The thickness should be mea-

sured, and measured again at a different site to see how regular the bed is. If it contains current bedding or sole marks, some attempt should be made to determine the direction of the current.

As with any bedded sequence, the folding should be noted and the orientation of the folds marked on your map. Likewise note the angle, the throw, and the orientation of any fault – faults are easier to see in bedded rocks than in unbedded. All this information will help you to understand the deformation that has taken place since the beds were laid down.

FINE-GRAINED SEDIMENTARY ROCKS

The finest sedimentary rocks are the shales, mudstones, and clays. They may be clastic or chemical sedimentary rocks, but are usually a mixture of both.

Mineralogy

The fine particles of these rocks may include fragments broken from preexisting rocks, such as quartz and, less commonly, feldspar and mica. There may be concentrations of rarer minerals such as zircon ($ZrSiO_4$).

Most particles, however, are of substances formed by the breakdown of other minerals. These include the clay minerals such as kaolinite ($Al_2(Si_2O_5)(OH)_4$) – the mineral from which china clay is made – and minerals that are akin to mica. These form a kind of a paste or an amorphous groundmass that is difficult to study.

Landscape and structures

These fine-grained rocks may form in the deep oceans or they may form in river beds, estuaries, and deltas. Each occurrence produces a different outcrop.

Those from deep oceans tend to form very thick sequences. They will probably contain fossils of deep-sea animals, or of animals that lived in the upper waters and sank after death. A soft muddy surface is very susceptible to markings, and so you may find sole marks or groove casts where blocks of debris have been dragged along the ocean floor by the currents, plowing through the top layer of ooze.

Occasionally any limy material present organizes itself into discrete layers after deposition to produce an alternating sequence of limestone and shale beds, such as the Jurassic Lias of England.

Shallow-water fine-grained sediments are usually found interbedded with sandstone and other sedimentary rocks, often in a cyclical sequence. When this happens, the fine-grained rock, being much softer than the sandstone, will be eroded first, leaving the harder beds jutting out as ledges. Fossils are often abundant, and the friable nature of the rock makes them easy to collect.

Nodules may be present. These form when a chemical in the sediment, such as silica, carbonate, or pyrite, gathers in a discrete mass and forms a lump at the same time that the sediment is turned to rock. They usually form flattened spheroids that lie in the plane of the bedding. Septarian nodules are worth looking for. These have a radial pattern of cracks filled with yet another mineral.

As with any bedded sedimentary rock, measure the thicknesses of the beds, determine the direction of strike and the angle of dip. Note any folds or faults.

Right The fine-grained sedimentary rocks are usually very soft compared with any other rocks in the area. Where clays, mudstones, or shales are interbedded with limestone, the beds of limestone are left protruding as shelves or ridges while the intervening fine material is washed away. This gives a deceptive step-like appearance to any cliff, although its unstable nature forbids any climbing.

Hand specimen Fine-grained sedimentary rocks are so soft that specimens are easily obtained.

When the rock can be split easily into thin brittle sheets, it is a shale. When it breaks into lenticular flakes, it is a mudstone. When it has little internal structure but is plastic and slippery when wet, it is a clay. If the distinction is not obvious when you hammer off a hand specimen, then apply the blade of a penknife and see how the specimen splits.

Fossils are likely to be present and these are most easily seen in shale because it spilts along the bedding plane where fossils are usually aligned. Fossils of marine animals are found in deep-sea shales; freshwater shellfish and plants lie in shallow-water shales.

Very dark marine shales can be rich in carbon, showing that they were deposited in a region deficient in oxygen (otherwise the carbon would have been incorporated into limestone or given off as carbon dioxide). Fossils in such shales may be of animals that suffocated after being swept into these regions by currents. The lack of oxygen leads to the formation of iron pyrites, and this may be present as crystals or as a replacement mineral in fossils.

Clay

Mudstone

Shale

centimeters

inches

Varieties Within the divisions of shale, mudstone, and clay, there are many different types. They are usually given names that are based on their economic importance.

China clay or kaolin is a white clay formed by the decomposition of the feldspars in granite.

Fuller's earth is a clay made from very fine volcanic ash, used for removing grease from wool.

Alum shale contains minerals that can be worked for alum.

Microscopic specimen Don't bother. The constituent fragments are too fine for the technique to be of any use.

SLATE

Slate is a low-grade metamorphic rock formed by the regional metamorphism of a fine-grained rock such as shale or volcanic ash.

Mineralogy

As with most metamorphic rocks, the chemical composition of slate is similar to that of the original rock, but the constituents have been rearranged into different minerals. The most significant minerals produced are those that form thin flat crystals, like mica or chlorite, developed from the original clay minerals of the rock. Quartz is likely to be the other major constituent.

Landscape and structures

Being regional metamorphic rocks, slates tend to be found in mountainous areas. The rock cleaves into thin sheets because of the alignment of the minerals, and so it tends to weather in a splintery manner. Erosional forces open cracks in the rock parallel to the cleavage plane.

When the cleavage is perfectly flat, the slate can be quarried and used for roofing material or for billiard tables. As slate is found in large masses, slate quarries tend to be huge, eating away entire mountains in such rugged areas as North Wales and the Appalachians of eastern North America.

The direction in which slate splits has nothing to do with the bedding of the original rocks. In fact, in some slates you can see the original bedding cutting across the cleavage plane. The cleavage is entirely due either to the alignment of the minerals – true cleavage – or the alignment of closely spaced microscopic folds – false cleavage, fracture cleavage, or strain-slip cleavage. The alignment corresponds to the direction of applied pressure as the rock metamorphosed.

Through strain markers it is sometimes possible to see the extent of the deformation. These are recognizable objects that have been distorted by the forces that changed the rock, and can include fossils and spherical pebbles.

Since you will usually be studying slates in mountainous areas, you should be sure to wear suitable clothes and shoes.

Note the direction of cleavage, and whether or not it is even for as much of the outcrop as you can see. If the direction varies from place to place, there may have been more than one phase of deformation – mountain-building movements metamorphosed the rock, and then more mountain-building movements distorted the metamorphosed rock.

Right Slate tends to form mountains, being produced by the regional metamorphic processes that accompany mountain-building. The rock was once valuable as a roofing material and for other industrial purposes, and so slate areas tend to have quarries and quarry towns in them, such as here in north Wales. Changing economic factors mean that now many of these quarries are disused and the towns run down.

Hand specimen Slate tends to be a fairly even rock, and being fine-grained a small sample is usually representative of the whole emplacement. Its color is usually a dark gray but, according to the precise mineral content, it can be green, blue, or reddish-brown. A hand lens may reveal the mica flakes that give the rock its cleavage, but often they are too small.

Varieties As with all rocks that have a commercial significance, there are several types recognized by their appearance. They vary in color according to their mineralogical makeup and some may have largish crystals scattered throughout, giving the slate a spotted appearance.

Similar rocks If slate continues to be subjected to the forces that produced the metamorphic effect, the grade of metamorphism will increase and produce phyllite – the next stage in the process. Phyllite is very similar to slate but the crystals are much larger, the shiny plates of mica being visible to the naked eye.

Even further pressure will develop the next stage of rock – schist.

inches

centimeters

Welsh slate

Microscopic specimen Through the microscope it is easy to see whether the cleavage is true or false. The former will show itself by the alignment of minerals, while the latter will present a wavy texture in the fine groundmass. Strain markers are visible on the microscopic scale as well. Tiny robust fragments and crystals that have resisted the metamorphism may be at the centers of eye-like structures. The matrix appears to have been pulled out away from the fragment in the direction of cleavage and the spaces so formed filled in by chlorite or quartz, like a miniature augen.

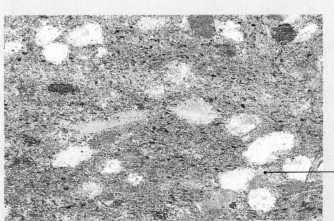

Chiastolite – an unusual form of andalusite (aluminum silicate) crystals in cross-shaped arrangements

45

SCHIST

Schist is a medium-grade regional metamorphic rock. It is found in ancient rock systems, where there were once mountains which have subsequently been eroded to stumps or to flat plains.

Mineralogy

The minerals in schist vary greatly, depending on the nature of the original rock and the circumstances of the metamorphism. Mica is nearly always present. A large proportion of mica suggests that the original rock was a fine-grained shale or mudstone. Less mica and more quartz and feldspar suggests a parent rock of sandstone. The presence of calcite shows that the original rock was limestone. Talc in a schist reveals that it formed from a basic igneous rock.

New minerals appear under conditions of increasing temperature and pressure. Geologists can identify these minerals and use them to determine the grade of metamorphism. Mica develops with light metamorphism. Then comes garnet mixed in with the mica. Then staurolite ($FeAl_4Si_2O_{10}(OH)_2$) – a yellow-colored mineral often with a cross-shaped twinned crystal. Then kyanite (Al_2SiO_5), which may form pale blue crystals. The final grade is signaled by the appearance of colorless fibrous crystals of sillimanite (with the same chemical formula as kyanite). Any further stress and the rock turns to gneiss or begins to melt.

Landscape and structures

A schist terrain has been greatly eroded. When you see outcrops of schist, you can tell that vast volumes of rock have been worn away in order to reveal them.

Like slate, schist is made up of flat minerals that have been aligned parallel to one another, and, like slate, it splits and weathers along these planes. However, schist cleavage planes are very irregular, undulating, and twisted. The whole range of tectonic structures – anticlines, synclines, thrusts, faults – can be seen affecting the cleavage. Mullions may develop, in which case mica may be formed around the outside of each of the cylindrical structures. The contorted nature of any outcrop will show the complex history of the area, with one phase of metamorphism and distortion superimposed on another. The most obvious direction of deformation is the one that was produced last. It may obliterate all the early ones.

Left Jagged mountain peaks are typical of schist terrain. The cleavage planes caused by the layers of mica in the rock mean that it is vulnerable to physical weathering and splits easily. Schist mountains are easily attacked by frost and form spectacular rugged scenery. The micas themselves may cause schist rocks to gleam and sparkle in the sunlight.

Hand specimen Hammer a specimen from the outcrop. It will split away along the cleavage plane. The presence of this splitting direction is so typical of schist that the term schistosity may be used about any rock, schist or otherwise, that shows it. In the United States the term foliation is used instead, but in other parts of the world foliation means the separation of minerals into discrete bands, as in gneiss.

The broken face of a hand specimen of schist will sparkle in the sun because of the mica crystals. The crystals may be big enough to be seen with the naked eye, but if not you will definitely see them with a hand lens. The other minerals, particularly the index minerals that show the grade of metamorphism, should be looked for too. Garnets will be readily recognizable by their deep red color and their other properties, and kyanite should be obvious by its light blue color. The other index minerals may be difficult to detect without trained help.

Varieties The many varieties of schist are the result of differences in the parent rock, and the grade of metamorphism.

Mica schists are the most common.

Calc-schist, with a high proportion of calcium, is derived from the metamorphism of limestone.

Greenschist, with a high proportion of the green mineral chlorite, is derived from basic igneous rocks.

Quartzo-feldspathic schist comes from metamorphism of sandstone.

inches

centimeters

Microscopic specimen A microscopic view of schist should show the schistosity by the alignment of the minerals, particularly of the micas. The presence of garnet should be obvious, and sometimes the well-formed garnet crystals are encased in an eye-shaped lens of quartz. Staurolite, if present, may show itself by large cross-shaped crystals.

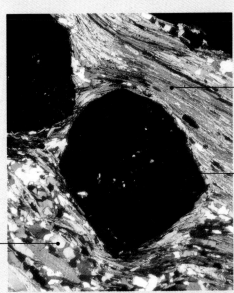

Mica – brightly colored and showing the strain of the formation

Garnet – isotropic therefore dark under crossed polars

Small quartz grains

47

PREPARING A FIELD NOTEBOOK

Your field notebook must be sturdy and have a hard, and preferably water-resistant, cover. There is nothing worse than standing in the rain trying to fill in information on soggy pages that are falling out of their binding – and watching the ink run because you brought the wrong kind of pen as well as the wrong kind of notebook.

It is not a good idea to take rough notes in the field and write them up afterward. Rough notes tend to be ambiguous, and their actual meaning becomes lost if you try to reconstruct your observations later. Write down as much as possible while you are on site and while the rocks and structures are there in front of you.

The entries in your field notebook must be comprehensible to you if you want to go back to the site a few years later, or if you give the notebook to another geologist who wants to follow up your work in the same area.

First you must record the location of your site. In the United States this means using a U.S.G.S. (United States Geological Survey) quadrangle map.

Make plenty of illustrations in your field notebook. One picture is worth a thousand words of description. Besides pictures of outcrops, sketch-maps of the sites are also useful.

More detailed sketches can be made on separate large sheets of paper, attached to your map case, and more information can be put on your field map.

All these can be put together to produce a comprehensive picture of the geology of an area, and can all be referred to when you write your final report.

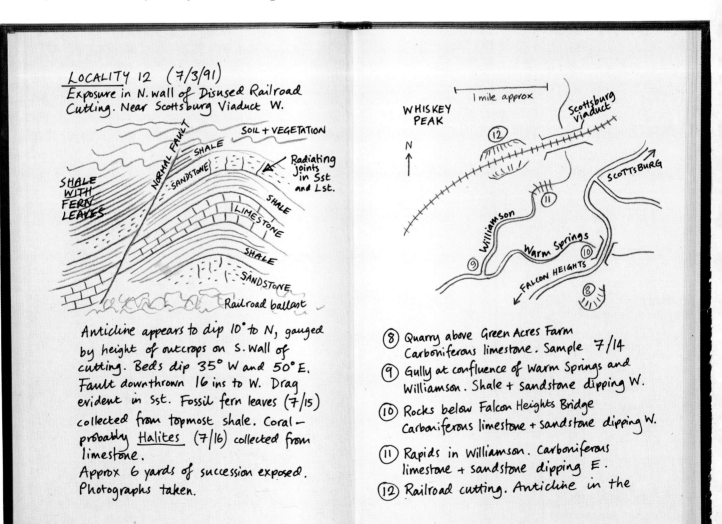

LOCALITY 12 (7/3/91)
Exposure in N. wall of Disused Railroad Cutting. Near Scottsburg Viaduct W.

SOIL + VEGETATION
NORMAL FAULT
SHALE
SANDSTONE
Radiating joints in Sst and Lst.
SHALE WITH FERN LEAVES
SHALE
LIMESTONE
SHALE
SANDSTONE
Railroad ballast

Anticline appears to dip 10° to N, gauged by height of outcrops on S. wall of cutting. Beds dip 35° W and 50° E. Fault downthrown 16 ins to W. Drag evident in sst. Fossil fern leaves (7/15) collected from topmost shale. Coral – probably Halites (7/16) collected from limestone.
Approx 6 yards of succession exposed.
Photographs taken.

WHISKEY PEAK
N
1 mile approx
Scottsburg Viaduct
12
Scottsburg
Williamson
11
Warm Springs
10
9
FALCON HEIGHTS
8

⑧ Quarry above Green Acres Farm Carboniferous limestone. Sample 7/14

⑨ Gully at confluence of Warm Springs and Williamson. Shale + sandstone dipping W.

⑩ Rocks below Falcon Heights Bridge Carboniferous limestone + sandstone dipping W.

⑪ Rapids in Williamson. Carboniferous limestone + sandstone dipping E.

⑫ Railroad cutting. Anticline in the